JOHNSON'S
BREXIT
DICTIONARY

Pushkin Press

HARRY EYRES & GEORGE MYERSON

JOHNSON'S BREXIT
DICTIONARY
OR, AN A TO Z OF WHAT
BREXIT <u>REALLY</u> MEANS

Leabharlanna Poiblí Chathair Baile Átha Cliath
Dublin City Public Libraries

Pushkin Press
71–75 Shelton Street
London WC2H 9JQ

First published by Pushkin Press in 2018

1 3 5 7 9 8 6 4 2

ISBN 13: 978-1-78227-498-8

Designed and typeset by Tetragon, London
Printed and bound by CPI Group (UK) Ltd, Croydon CR0 4YY

www.pushkinpress.com

Dedicated to the immortal memory of

SAMUEL JOHNSON

*Poet, critic, essayist, biographer,
lexicographer, editor*

*Born Lichfield 18th September 1709
Died London 13th December 1784*

'As any opinion grows popular it will innovate speech
in the same proportion as it alters practice'

SAMUEL JOHNSON, Preface to
A Dictionary of the English Language

'Patriotism is the last refuge of a scoundrel'

Remark made by Samuel Johnson on the evening of 7th April 1775.
Recorded by James Boswell, his friend and biographer.

Preface

Brexit is a lexicographer's nightmare. After all, the best definition the person responsible for carrying through this enormity has been able to devise is a circular one: 'Brexit means Brexit.' Brexit may in fact mean many things, but none of them is clear: a negotiating process in which no real negotiating ever gets done; a promise of trade deals which somehow fail to materialize; the taking back of control leading to ever-intensifying chaos; or a play by Samuel Beckett in which the main character never arrives.

Fortunately a saviour is at hand. We have been able to enlist the help of the great eighteenth-century lexicographer and polymath Dr Samuel Johnson – the man who heroically and single-handedly, in response to the efforts of the entire French Academy, created the first comprehensive, illustrated dictionary of the English language. Johnson's *Dictionary* is one of the landmark accomplishments not only of English but of world literature, a work whose scholarship and lexicography, though of course dated, are still often enlightening and whose wit, wisdom and eloquence are no more past their read-by date than *Hamlet* or *Pride and Prejudice*.

Johnson's Brexit Dictionary gives us the pithy, incisive and sometimes opinionated definitions of the key terms associated with this momentous process which Samuel Johnson would have added to his classic *Dictionary of the English Language*, had he been preparing a new edition in 2018. These new definitions sit alongside original ones, which illuminate our current quandaries and predicament in surprising ways.

Politically, we can only guess what Johnson would have made of Brexit. He was a devout Anglican and a staunch Tory; also a man of surprisingly liberal and forward-looking views on many subjects. He loved to insult the Scots and the French, but at the same time he admired many aspects of Scottish society and would never have undertaken the *Dictionary* if he had not wished to emulate the French Academy. Above all, he was no British bulldog but a European scholar, a student of many languages and disciplines, intimately versed in all the intellectual currents of the continent.

In his original preface, Johnson lamented the fate of the lexicographer, never appreciated for his or her invaluable work in mapping out the terrain of the language and making comprehensible what was once a 'wild and barbarous jargon', but only blamed for mistakes. We do not doubt that this will be our fate also.

ABSURD.

Unreasonable; without judgement, as used of people and in Brexit disputes, suggesting charms as much as folly, or the charm of folly.

'you had better take for business a man somewhat absurd, than over formal' (BACON)

'the voters did prefer the Leave campaign, though somewhat absurd, to the Remain campaign, for it was over formal' (BACKON)

'Credo quia absurdum.'

(LATIN PRINCIPLE OF FAITH)

'It's a bit absurd, so I kind of believe it.'

(BREXIT PRINCIPLE OF FAITH)

ADJOURNMENT.

[*adjournment*, French] An assignment of a day, or a putting off till another day.

'We will, and we will not, and then we will not again, and we will. At this rate we run our lives out in adjournments from time to time, out of a fantastical levity that holds us off and on, betwixt hawk and buzzard.' (L'ESTRANGE)

'The Brexit deal will be an adjournment – the easiest thing in human history.' (PSEUDO-FOX)

'The Brexit talks were adjourned once again.'

(SPOKESPERSON FOR M. BARNIER)

AFFIDAVIT.

Signifies in the language of the common law that he made oath; a declaration upon oath. Hence, currently, *to Daffidavis*, to swear a wild oath in the manner of Daffidavis, agent for Brexit abroad, as 'He Daffidavised that he would not make any compromise.'

AGREEMENT.

Concord. A feature rarely found in the world of Brexit.

'What agreement is there between the hyena and the dog?'
(ECCLESIASTES VIII.18)

'What agreement is there between Mr Fox and the frogs?'
(YE DAILY CHAIN MAIL)

ALECONNER.

An official in the city of London, whose business is to inspect the measures of publick houses.

One who seeks to deceive by drinking ale or being seen drinking ale, as 'Sir Boris hath not a half of Master Nigel's skill as an aleconner.' (Shakespeare, Henry IV Part VIII)

ALGORITHM.

Used to imply the six operations of arithmetic, or the science of numbers, and latterly, occult influences that both reveal and shape the future.

'Once upon a day, it was ye Sonne wot won it for Sir Major, but now 'tis the algorithms that do win all.'
(LORD BERNERS-LEE)

*'Master Soothsayer, tell us what the algorithms do say,
prithee do!'*   (SHAKESPEARE, BORIUS CAESAR)

AMEND.

To correct; to change anything wrong to something better; a key word in the parliamentary turmoil over Brexit.

'Amend your ways and your doings.'
                              (JEREMIAH VII.3)

'Amend your Brexit bill and your doings.'
                              (AH JEREMY XXX.1)

Amendment, a change from the bad for the better.

*'some things in it have passed your approbation and
amendment'*   (DRYDEN)

*'A multitude of things in this Brexit bill be so bad that
the less bad counts for an amendment still.'*
                              (ADDIDSON)

ANATIFEROUS.

Producing ducks. So, **BREXANATIFEROUS**, producing dead ducks, which quack loudly ne'ertheless.

ANCHENTRY.

Antiquity of a family; ancient dignity; the part of the populace that widely voted for Brexit.

ANGER.

Uneasiness or discomposure of the mind, upon the receipt of any injury, with a present purpose of revenge. A currently much-favoured emotion.

'Anger is, according to some, a transient hatred, or at least very like it.' (SOUTH)

'Brexit is, according to some, a transient anger, or at least very like it.' (NORTH)

ARMADA.

[a fleet of war, Spanish] An armament for sea; anything Spanish in the popular news-sheets; by extension, any European Union action or proposal viewed with disfavour by Brexiteers.

'an Armada of European regulations'
(YE DAILY CHAIN MAIL)

'the Euro armada of red tape'
(THE DAILY DEPRESSED)

ARRANT.

[Uncertain etymology, but probably from *errant*, which being at first applied in its proper signification to vagabonds, as an *errant* or *arrant rogue*, that is, a *rambling rogue*, lost, in time, its original signification, and, being by its use understood to imply something bad, was applied at large to any thing that was mentioned with hatred or contempt.] Bad in high degree.

'A vain fool grows forty times an arranter sot than before.'   (L'Estrange's Fables)

Hence *arrant* as epithet for a knave who delivers rambling rants, as 'Arrant Banks held forth afresh on Brexit.'   (Addidson)

ASLEEP.

Sleeping; at rest; hence undisturbed by any concern for action or events.

'How many thousands of my poorest subjects Are at this hour asleep!'   (Shakespeare)

'How many of my poorest ministers Are at this hour asleep!'

(Good Mistress May,
in Shakespeare, daft folio)

BAA.

The cry of a sheep.

BACKFRIEND.

A friend backwards; that is, an enemy in secret. So also in our recent politicks, *frontfriend*, 'Messrs Gove and Johnson were firm frontfriends.'

BACKWARDS.

From the present station to the place beyond the back; regressively. Towards something past. From a better to a worse state. Perversely; from the wrong end. So, **BREXWARDS**, regressing perversely to a worse, past state.

BARN, BARNIER.

A place or house for laying up any sort of grain, hay or straw. Hence a *barnier*, one who has a plentiful supply of last straws after all others have run out.

'Prithee Master Barnier, dost have some straw for mine ass?'

'Tush, Master Daffidavis, 'tis my last straw but thou mayst have it for thine ass.'

(BEN JONSON, BARTHOLOMEW MARKET)

In the current popular news-sheets, this word has led to some mirthful play upon the name of Monsieur Barnier, agent of France and other powers in these Brexit affairs (a name which has as a further indignity sometimes alternatively been punned with 'Barmier', after the cant and low word *barmy*).

BEEFEATER.

The business of the beefeaters was, and perhaps still is, to attend the king at meals, and also to promote British gin between meals; also where Brexit is at issue generally, a great patriot claims to be a huge eater of beef and so beefeater.

'Thou art not so great a beefeater as I!'

(MASTER NIGEL SHALLOW,
IN SHAKESPEARE, HENRY IV PART IV)

BEER.

[*bir*, Welsh] Liquor made of malt and hops. It is distinguished from ale, either by being older or smaller, and for Brexit purposes it is distinguished from mere continental lager by being warm and flat.

'Here's a pot of good double beer'

(SHAKESPEARE, HENRY VI PART II)

'Hast thou a treble pot of beer, good sirrah?'

(MASTER NIGEL SHALLOW,
IN SHAKESPEARE, HENRY IV PART VI)

BESPOKE.

[from *to bespeak*] To order or entreat anything beforehand, or against a future time, as

'Here is the cap your worship did bespeak'
(SHAKESPEARE, THE TAMING OF THE SHREW)

Hence *bespoke*, having been entreated before-hand or against a future time, exactly as required; customized for order; on demand; personally requested.

'Here is thy most bespoke Brexit
An't please thy ladyship, prithee'

(SHAKESPEARE,
THE TAMING OF THE EU, DOUBTFUL FOLIO)

BIBACITY.

The quality of drinking much.

An effusion of animal spirits in the City of London occasioned by much drinking of champagne.

BIDENTAL.

Having two teeth, hence a bit better than tooth-less but not much, as of our current Brexit agents.

'Daffidavis, though not toothless in the negotiations, was at best bidental.'

(ADDIDSON)

BIGOTRY.

The practice or tenet of a bigot; violently inhumane prejudice habitually expressed as if it were normal, a tendency that some do find enhanced by Brexit.

'Our silence makes our adversaries think we persist in those bigotries which all good and sensible men despise.'
(POPE)

'Our silence in speaking out makes everyone think we persist in those bigotries which all good and sensible people despise.'
(HOPE)

BILL. (1)

An account of money; in the case of Brexit, a somewhat amplified account.

'Ordinary expense ought to be limited by a man's estate, and ordered to the best, that the bills may be less than the estimation abroad.'
(BACON)

'It did transpire that the bill for Brexit was somewhat considerably greater than the estimation both abroad and at home.'
(BACKON)

'Voici ze bill, s'il vous plaît.'
(M. BARMIER TO DAFFIDAVIS)

BILL. (2)

A law presented to the parliament but not yet made an act; a phase much dwelt upon in Brexit.

*'How now for mitigation of this bill
Urg'd by the commons?'*   (SHAKESPEARE, HENRY V)

*'What mitigation of this Brexit bill
Splurged by the commons?'*

(SHAKESPEARE, PECULIAR FOLIO)

BIN.

A place where bread or corn or wine is reposited. Hence *Cor-bin*, a place where Corbyns are reposited in the wishful dreams of some Brexiteer pundits.

'The most convenient way of picking hops, is into a long square frame of wood, called a bin.'   (MORTIMER)

'The most convenient way of depositing Corbyns, is into a long square frame of wood, called a Cor-bin.'

(YE BRIGHT SHINY SONNE)

BISCUIT.

[from *bis*, twice, Latin, and *cuit*, baked, French]
A kind of hard, dry bread made to be carried to sea: it is baked for long voyages four times.

'Many have been cured of dropsies by abstinence from drinks, eating dry biscuit, which creates no thirst.'

(ARBUTHNOT)

Hence too **BREXSCUIT**, a kind of hard, dry Brexit half-baked eight times and thus made to carry on for months and months before being swallowed with great difficulty by a reluctant publick.

BLACKMAIL.

A certain rate of money, corn, cattle or other consideration, paid to men allied with robbers, to be by them protected from the danger of such as usually rob or steal. A certain rate of money, corn, cattle or other consideration demanded, so the news-sheets say, by the European Union as the price for Brexit.

'EU Brexit Blackmail' (YE DAILY CHAIN MAIL)

BLUNDER.

To mistake grossly; to err very widely.

'Someone had blundered.'

(ALFRED, LORD TENNYSON,
'THE CHARGE OF THE BREXIT BRIGADE')

BLUSTROUS.

[from *bluster*] Tumultuous; noisy; a feature of Brexit-favouring orators.

'The ancient heroes were illustrious
For being benign, and not blustrous.'   (HUDIBRAS)

'The Brexiteers were more industrious
Than the Remainers, and far more blustrous.'

(LUDICRAS)

BOHEA.

A species of tea, of higher colour, and more astringent taste, than green tea. Hence a *Boheamian*, one who lives mainly on bohea, and having the characteristics of one always full of bohea.

'Be aware that the British, though outwardly respectable,
do lead a shockingly Boheamian life.'

(YE GUIDE BOOKE FOR TOURISTES
TO THE UNITED KINGEDOME)

BORDER.

The outer part or edge of anything; the edge of a country, the confine.

'How may we border upon control, Master Nigel, if we do not control our border?' 'Tush, Sir Boris, 'tis sure the reverse, nay, fie upon such wranglings! They do ache my brains! Pass the ale!'

(SHAKESPEARE, HENRY VII
PART VII, FUDGED FOLIO)

Hence also *to border*, to touch something at the side or edge.

'It bordereth upon the province of Croatia.'

(KNOLLES)

'Scotland, alas, doth border upon England and England doth border upon madness.'

(THE TRUE SCOTS SALMON)

BOTS.

A species of small worms found in the entrails of horses. Virtual worms which infect the body politic.

BOUTISALE.

A sale at a cheap rate, as booty or plunder is commonly sold.

'To speak nothing of the great boutisale of colleges and chantries.'

(HAYWARD)

'To speak nothing of the great boutisale of our news and media networks.'   (PAYWARD)

Hence *boutique sale*, a chic and apparently cheap sale at a fashionable shop or, by extension, any such reduced-price offer for posh-seeming items.

'There was this last few years a fine boutique sale of exclusive seats in the House of Lords to wealthy donors.'
(WAYWARD)

Hence also *car-boutisale*, a lower and more popular pursuit in which a person's or a country's effects can be bought and sold for nearly nothing.

BOZZA.

Botch [from *bozza*, pronounced '*botza*', Italian] A part of any work ill-finished, so as to appear worse than the rest.

Botcher [from Botch] A mender of old clothes.

Bozza [Bo'zza] One who attempts to patch up a political career in tatters, as 'Sir Boris was well-named by the soubriquet "Bozza", for he did patch his career together from rags and shreds.' (Addidson)

BREXIT.

Exit. The term set in the margin of plays to mark the time at which the player goes off stage. Recess; departure; act of quitting the stage; act of quitting the theatre of life. Passage out of any place; way by which there is a passage out.

   BREXIT. The term set in the margin of history to mark the time at which Britain wanders towards the edge of the stage. Act of trying to quit the stage of history. A desired but elusive exit from Europe, as 'Though the ministry looked long and hard, they could not find the Brexit.'

   And hence also *exitious*. [from exitial] Destructive, fatal, mortal, deleterious.

   BREXITIAL. Destructive and leading to Brexit. Used of things that result in Brexit, as 'Mr Davis played a very Brexitial role.'

   BREXITIOUS. As annoying as Brexit, as 'the whole day was really Brexitious'. Also used of those full of enthusiasm for Brexit, as 'The paper was always extremely Brexitious.'

BRRRM-BRRRM.

The cry of a motor-car.

BUBBLE.

A small bladder of water; a cheat; a false show. Anything which wants solidity and firmness, such as the overblown hopes of an easy Brexit.

'Directors' promises but wind,
South-sea, at best, a mighty bubble'   (SWIFT)

'Chancellors' promises but wind,
Brexit, at best, a mighty bubble'   (RATHER-TOO-SWIFT)

'Estate agents' promises but wind,
House prices, at best, a mighty bubble'
                                        (PRETTY-DAMN-SWIFT)

BUFFOON.

A man whose profession is to make sport by low jests and antick-postures; a jack-pudding; one employed to make a mirthful entertainment of Brexit with low jests and antick-postures; a hack-pudding.

'Ah, Sir Boris, 'tis said I am a jester
But thou art the right buffoon.'

                            (MASTER NIGEL SHALLOW,
                                      IN SHAKESPEARE,
                               PRINCE HARRY V PART V)

BULLDOG.

[from *bull* and *dog*] A dog of a particular form, remarkable for his courage. He is used in baiting the bull; and this species is so peculiar to Britain, that they are said to degenerate when they are carried to other countries.

'All the harmless part of him is that of a bulldog; they are tame no longer than they are not offended.'
(ADDISON)

'All the harmless part of him is that of a bulldog; he is calm no longer than he is not offended, and he does take ready offence, notably with Monsieur Barmier.'
(ADDIDSON ON JOHNSON)

BUMBARD.

A great gun; a loud and terrible poet or ranting author.

'It is much to be feared that this Brexit will arouse the unwelcome clamour of loud bumbards and shrieking twitterers.'
(ADDIDSON)

BUREAU, BUREAUCRACY.

A chest of drawers with a writing-board; hence, by extension, *bureaucracy*, rule by those who possess a chest of drawers with a writing-board whereupon to draft petty regulations. A condition of rule once supposed to be remedied by Brexit, which, however, turns out to require vast numbers of British writing-boards and many thousands of home-cooked regulations.

BUSINESS.

Employment; multiplicity of affairs; serious engagement, in opposition to trivial trans-actions; a word much bandied in our Brexit disputes.

'Must business thee from hence remove?'   (DONNE)

'Must Brexit thy business from here remove?'
(DONE)

Also *to do one's business*, to kill, destroy or ruin him.

'It is much feared among those of business that this Brexit will do their business entirely.'
(SIR RICHARD STEAL)

CHANNEL.

A strait or narrow sea between two countries, as the British Channel, between Britain and France; also *official channel*, a strait and narrow means of communication kept open with difficulty between Britain and Europe, also known as Monsieur Barmier.

CHAPELLANY.

[from *chapel*] Does not subsist within itself but built within and founded upon some other church. A miscellaneous collection of chaps that does not subsist within itself but is dependent upon some other party, as many do say is so of the government of our Brexit time.

'This Brexifying government is a mere chapellany and no self-sufficient power.'   (ADDIDSON)

CHAT, CHATBOT.

Idle talk, prate.

'Snuff, or the fan, supplies each pause of chat,
With singing, laughing, ogling, and all that.' (POPE)

Hence *chatbot*, device for the production of idle talk or chat, much suspected of being employed to contrive such *chatter* and idle talk favourable to Brexit.

'Staff, or the bot, supplies each pause of chat,
With lying, jeering, Brexit, and all that.'   (POP)

Hence also **BREXBOT**, a device for the automatic and mechanical production of Brexit.

CHATTERING (CLASSES).

[from *chatter*, to make a noise as a pie, or other unharmonious bird] Hence *chattering*, making an unharmonious noise, as *chattering classes*, that class of society from whom emanates a constant noise which many find unharmonious and antagonising, leading, some have said, to the loud 'no' of Brexit.

'Truly the coffee-house folk and chattering classes did talk themselves unwittingly out of Europe, so much did they provoke the other kinds of people by their incessant clamours.'

(ADDIDSON)

CHIMERA, CHIMERICAL.

A vain and wild fancy as remote from reality as the existence of the poetical chimera, a monster feigned to have head of a lion, the belly of a goat and the tail of a dragon.

'Mr Fox's fancies of trade deals turned out to be purely chimerical.'

(SIR RICHARD STEAL)

'Sign up for a good British chimera.'

(SIR BORIS DE JOHNSON)

COCK (UP).

To strut, to hold up the head, and look big or menacing or pert.

'Everyone cocks and struts upon it.'   (ADDISON)

Hence *to cock up*, to hold the head up extra high and look extremely big or menacing or very pert indeed.

'Let us not be downcast, my Daffidavis,
But cock up bravely, good sirrah.'

(SIR BORIS, IN SHAKESPEARE,
HENRY VIII PART VII)

COLD.

Not hot, not warm; without warmth, without heat.

Unaffected, frigid. Unaffecting, unable to move the passions.

Reserved, coy; not affectionate, not cordial, not friendly.

Not welcome; not received with kindness or warmth of affection.

''Twas a cold May, which did freeze the buds right off.'

(SHAKESPEARE, AS YOU LIKE IT NOT)

COMMIGRATE.

To remove in a body or by consent from one country to another.

To share and support the journey of migrants, to consent gladly to the arrival of migrants.

COMMISSIONER (EUROPEAN).

A person included in a warrant of authority; one who is commissioned by a commission to fulfil a commission.

'A commissioner is one who hath commission.'

(COWELL)

'These commissioners came into England, with whom covenants were concluded.' (HAYWARD)

Hence a *European Commissioner* is one who is commissioned by a European Commission to fulfil a commission for Europe.

'A European Commissioner is one who hath commission to perform a commission for Europe from the European Commission.'

(CROWELL, RULES OF THE EUROPEAN COMMISSION, A BOOK COMMISSIONED BY THE EUROPEAN COMMISSION)

COMPROMISE.

A compact or bargain, in which some concessions are made on each side. Sometimes employed as a term of British virtue, but at others, and especially where Brexit is concerned, used as a term of contempt implying craven surrender.

'Wars have not wasted it, for warr'd he hath not,
But basely yielded, upon compromise'

(SHAKESPEARE, RICHARD II)

'Warr'd we have not,
But basely Brexited, upon compromise'

(SHAKESPEARE, DAFFIDAVIS II, STRANGE QUARTO)

CONTRIBUTE.

To give to some common stock; to advance towards some common design; especially used of Britain with regard to Europe, to give more than everyone else to a common design.

'England contributes much more than any other of the allies.' (ADDISON)

'Britain has contributed much more than any of the other member states.' (ADDIDSON)

Hence also *contribution*, that which is given by several hands for some common purpose, and hence *British contribution*, an unfairly excessive contribution.

'Beggars are now maintained by voluntary contributions.' (GRAUNT)

'The other states are now maintained by British contributions.' (SIR HECTOR GRUNT, KC, OMG)

CORBAN.

An alms-basket; a receptacle of charity.

'Thoud'st make of this nation one vast Corban, if thou could'st, sirrah Corbyn, ha ha!'

(SIR BORIS, IN BEN JONSON, BARTHOLOMEW UNFAIR)

CORNY.

Horny; scrawny; yawny.

'the corny reed' (MILTON)

'the corny screed of the news-sheets' (ADDIDSON)

COSMOPOLITAN.

A citizen of the world; one who is at home in every place, except possibly in Britain during its more insular or Brexit moods.

Also *cosmopolite*, being polite in a snooty kind of way, as 'Monsieur Barmier was extremely calm and cosmopolite during the negotiations.'

COST.

Charge; expense; notably an alarming feature of Brexit revealed surprisingly belatedly.

'I shall never hold that man my friend,
Whose tongue shall ask me for one penny cost.'

(SHAKESPEARE, HENRY IV)

'I shall never hold Barmier my friend
Whose tongue asks for a billion quid.'

(DAFFIDAVIS IN SHAKESPEARE,
HENRY IV PART IV, SCENE IN
BRUSSELS BAR FOUND ONLY IN THE
QUIRKY QUARTO AND THE FUSTY FOLIO)

COUGH.

[medical] A convulsion of the lungs, vellicated by some sharp serosity.

Politically, a device for obscuring the meaning of speech.

A cue for a standing ovation by purported allies, some quicker to their feet than others.

CRICKET.

A sport at which the contenders drive a ball with sticks or bats in opposition to each other. Seen as peculiarly British, though players from our former colonies and dominions have long surpassed our native batsmen and bowlers.

'The senator at cricket urge the ball.'   (POPE)

Hence *not cricket*, any sport at which the contenders do not drive a ball with sticks or bats in opposition to each other, as 'The conduct of Monsieur Barmier in the negotiations was just not cricket.' (Addidson)

CRISIS.

The point at which the disease kills or changes for the better; the point at which Brexit kills or changes for the better, oft delayed and much proclaimed.

'This hour's the very crisis of your fate.'   (DRYDEN)

'This hour's the very crisis of your Brexit.'   (DRYPEN)

CUSTOM(S).

Tribute; tax paid for goods imported or exported, and liable to rapid increase through Brexit.

'the escheats and forfeitures, the customs, butlerage, and imposts' (BACON)

'the cheats and forfeitures, the customs, butlerage, and imposts'

(RASHER, ON THE TERMS
OF THE TRADE ARRANGEMENTS FOR BREXIT)

'Butlerage' being the fee payable for keeping MPs' butlers, and 'imposts' the grant for the fixing of posts around ministers' gardens.

CYANTHROPY.

A species of madness in which men have the qualities of dogs. So, **BREXCYANTHROPY**, a species of madness in which men go barking, oft-times in Barking.

CYNICAL.

Having the qualities of a dog; currish, snarling; satirical; having little or no moral hesitancy in pursuing self-interest; notably a much-bandied accusation in our current travails on all sides.

'his cynical phrase' (WILKINS)

'his cynical view' (BILKINS)

'their cynical power-grab'
(DAILY DEPRESSED REPORT ON THE EUROPEAN UNION)

Hence also professional, as a *cynical foul* at football.

'That was a very cynical foul, very professional.'
(SPILIKINS)

DAMP.

Not completely dry; a distinctive feature of Britain and thus felt to justify Brexit from less damp Europe.

'This sceptred isle
Is also rather damp.'

(SHAKESPEARE, POOR QUARTO)

DANKISH.

Somewhat dank; also half-hearted Teutonic politeness (from the German *danken*, now meaning 'to thank', and originally, 'to make or be dank'), as 'Frau Merkel was dankish in her response to Mistress May's efforts.'

DESPATCH (BOX).

Hasty execution. Hence *despatch box* in the House of Commons, site of the speedy execution of ministers.

DISANNUL.

To void; to vacate; to nullify. This word is formed by those who, not knowing the meaning of the word *annul*, intended to form a negative sense by the needless use of the negative particle. On such grounds of wrongful prefixity, we might also object that some have coined 'to Brexit' not as meaning to exit *from* Britain, which it should truly be (as **BREXODUS**), but contrary to logic, 'to make a *British* exit' out of somewhere else, which makes little sense, not specifying whence.

DITCH (LAST).

A trench cut in the ground, usually between fields. Used of anything worthless, or thrown away into ditches. Hence *last-ditch*, thrown into the last or worst ditch, as has often been the case with current crises.

'The government has today made an attempt to rescue these most dilatory Brexit negotiations, but it is a most grim and last-ditch affair.' (ADDISON)

DIVISION.

Disunion; discord; difference, notably seen as both cause and consequence of Brexit.

'There was a division among the people.'
(JOHN VII.43)

'There was a division among the British people.'
(BREXIT VIII.47)

Also *first division*, former name for the topmost class of English football clubs, now corrupted into the most un-English 'Premiership'.

DIVORCE.

To force asunder; to separate by violence; to Brexitize apart.

'The continent and the island were continued together, within men's remembrance, by a drawbridge; but are now divorc'd by the downfallen cliffs.'   (CAREW)

'The continent and the island were continued together, within people's remembrance, by a drawbridge or union; but are now divorc'd by the uprisen referendum.'
(A-GNUTHER CAREW)

So, *divorce bill*, an enormous and contentious sum drawn up by lawyers.

DODDERED.

Overgrown with dodder; covered with super-crescent plants; inclined to vote for or be enthused about Brexit.

'dodder'd with age'   (DRYDEN)

'dodder'd with Brexit'   (DRYPEN)

DRAWBRIDGE.

A bridge made to be lifted up; to hinder or admit communication at pleasure; as a fancied drawbridge might have been uplifted to separate Britain from the continent.

'Half the buildings were raised on the continent, and the other half on an island, continued together by a drawbridge.' (CAREW)

'Half the publick œconomy was raised on the continent, and the other half on our island, continued together by a drawbridge until it was raised by Brexiteers.'

(ADAM SMYTH)

DULL.

Not exhilarating, not delightful; as to make dictionaries is dull work. So, *dEUll*, anything pertaining to the EU.

E.

Two sounds, long as in scene and short as in men or Brexit.

EARLESS.

Without any ears.

'Tush, good sir, 'tis but the Commons:
We are earless of them.'

(MISTRESS MAY, IN SHAKESPEARE, WONKY QUARTO)

ECLAT.

Splendour, show, lustre. Not English.

'Daffidavis's speech fell flat
Compared with Barmier's éclat.'   (ALEXANDER POP)

ELEPHANT (IN THE ROOM).

The largest of all quadrupeds, of whose sagacity, prudence and even understanding, many surprising relations are given. This animal feeds on hay, herbs and all sorts of pulse, and is said to be extremely long-lived. He is supplied with a trunk, of long, hollow cartilage, which hangs between his teeth, and serves him for hands. Hence the most conspicuous of beasts whose presence it is somewhat difficult to pass over, even should one wish to ignore it, as many currently are said to do.

'At this day's cabinet-council, they say that Brexit was
the elephant in the room.'   (NOT-TOO-SWIFT)

'Brexit is the elephant in the Euro Council room.'
(PRETTY-DAMN-SWIFT)

'When the cabinet meets, the Foreign Secretary, though
oft-times absent, is ever the elephant in the room.'
(ADDIDSON)

EMERGENCY.

The act of rising out of any fluid by which it is covered; unexpected casualty; pressing necessity, exigence; Brexit.

'In any case of emergency, he would employ the whole wealth of his empire.' (ADDISON)

'In any case of emergency, empty whole wealth of nation from this window.'
(BANK OF ENGLAND GUIDELINES FOR BREXIT POLICY)

ENEMY.

[of the people] A publick foe; a private opponent; a foe of the publick, as a judge who decides a question of law regarding Brexit in an unwanted manner, according to *Ye Daily Chain Mail*.

ENLARGEMENT.

Increase; augmentation; further extension, notably of the European Union.

'enlargement, or addition of earth, made to the continent'
(WOODWARD ON GEOLOGY)

'enlargement, or addition of earth, made to the continent'
(WOODWARD ON THE EUROPEAN UNION)

Enlarged, having an increased magnitude or extent, as 'M. Barmier showed signs of a somewhat enlarged ego as a consequence of the enlargement of the Continental Union.' (Addidson)

ENTITLE.

To give a claim to anything. Hence *entitled*, to have a natural claim to something; much brandished in current controversies.

'entitled to your heav'n, and rites divine'   (DRYDEN)

'he entitled himself'   (ATTERBURY)

'The Remain campaign did act as if it were entitled to our assent.'   (ADDIDSON)

'Master Cameron and Mr Osborne seem to think themselves entitled to the approbation of the populace.'   (BACKON)

'A fig for your entitlement!'   (SHAKESPEARE, SMUDGY QUARTO)

EULOGY.

Praise; encomium; panegyrick.

'the praises and famous eulogies of worthy men'

(SPENSER)

Hence *Eueulogy*, praise, encomium, panegyrick of the European Union; oft-times used with a measure of wit or sarcasm.

'An endless Eueulogy from M. Barmier'

(YE DAILY TELLOGRAPH)

EUPHONY.

An agreeable sound; a fake who works on behalf of the EU. Hence also *euphonious*.

EUTHANASIA.

An easy death. Strangulation by EU regulations, according to Brexiteers.

EXCISE.

A hateful tax levied upon commodities, and adjudged not by the common judges of property, but by wretches hired by those to whom excise is paid. So, **BREXCISE**, additional taxes and tariffs levied on all goods as a result of Brexit, as 'It was all a pointless Brex-er-cise.'

EXPERT.

Skilful; intelligent. Too oft used mistrustfully nowadays.

'Now will we take some order in the town,
Placing therein some expert officers.'

(SHAKESPEARE,
HENRY VI PART I)

'These officers are too expert by half.'
(SHAKESPEARE,
DOUBTFUL PAPERBACK EDITION)

'Thou art too expert for thine owne good, sirrah!'
(BEN JONSON, BARTHOLOMEW UNFAIR)

EXSUCTION.

The act of sucking out, or draining out, without immediate contact of the power sucking with the thing sucked, as has been much imputed may be the case with hidden influences on Brexit.

'If you open the valve, and force up the sucker, after this first exsuction you will drive out almost a whole cylinder full of air.'   (BOYLE)

Hence also **BREXSUCTION**, act of sucking Britain out of Europe and draining out, without immediate contact of the power sucking with the thing sucked, as

'There are strong suspicions around town of nefarious Muscovite plotters who through an artful Brexsuction have secretly and without trace drawn us from Europe.'
(ADDIDSON)

Thus also a **BREXSUCKEE**, one who has been Brexsucked.

FACTOTUM.

[*fac totum*, Latin; used likewise in burlesque French] A servant employed alike in all kinds of business. A 'researcher' employed to make up facts about all kinds of business, such as the millions of pounds per hour that will flow to the NHS after Brexit.

FAR-FETCH.

A deep stratagem; a ludicrous word. So, **FAR-BREXIT**, a ludicrous stratagem, couched in deep language.

FART.

Wind from behind.

'Love is the fart
Of every heart'   (SUCKLING)

'Brexit's the fart
Doth break my heart'   (DUCKLING)

FIB.

[a cant word among children] A lie; a falsehood, a term that has recently passed into political usage.

'Destroy his fib or sophistry; in vain,
The creature's at his dirty work again.'   (POPE)

'Many accuse Sir Boris of telling fibs, but he gives not a fig for them.'   (SIR OGDEN GNASH)

Hence also *to fib*, to tell falsehoods and *to ad-fib*, to improvise a lie, as

'Hast thou a lie prepar'd for all occasions, Sir Boris?'
'Nay, Master Shallow, I do but ad-fib occasionally. Do
not we all do so?'

(SHAKESPEARE, HENRY VII
PART VIII, QUIRKY FOLIO)

So also *FBI*, an agency accused by President
Trump of fibbing.

FINOCHIO.

A species of fennel; a plant, which is said to
grow in proportion as it senses a lie in the
vicinity.

'Sir Boris, how dost thou grow
Such fine finochio?'   (PSEUDO-HUDIBRAS)

FISHERY, FISHERIES.

The business of catching fish, much argued
over in the Brexit disputes, where not all are
blithe about the continued flourishing of this
enterprise.

'We shall have plenty of mackerel this season; our fishery
will not be disturb'd by privateers.'   (ADDISON)

'We shall have plenty of mackerel this season, unless our
fishery be disturb'd by Brexiteers.'   (ADDIDSON)

FISHY.

Consisting of fish; inhabited by fish; having the qualities or form of fish. Hence of anything that is somewhat slippery.

'the fishy flood' (POPE)

'the fishy claim that after Brexit all should be rich as Croesus' (SIR OGDEN NASHE)

*'Dost think, man, there be not something fishy
About Sir Boris?'*

*'Good lord, nay, he is honest as daylight:
Has told me so himself many a time,
And I do most heartily believe't.'*

(SHAKESPEARE, DODGY FOLIO)

FOOTBALL.

A ball commonly made of a blown bladder, cased with leather, driven by the foot. Latterly, a plastic ball, cased with technical jargon, driven by the outside of the right foot from just outside the area.

*'As when a sort of lusty shepherds try
Their force at football'* (WALLER)

'*As when a sort of hugely overpaid shepherds try
Their force at football*' (WALLY)

Hence also the sport or practice of *kicking the
football*, originally British but latterly not so
much, and thus emblematic of some of Britain's
declining status.

'*He was sensible the common football was a very imperfect imitation of that exercise.*'
(ARBUTHNOT AND POPE)

'*Dost agree the English football is a very imperfect
imitation of that exercise abroad, Master Shearer?*'
(THE FOOTBALL SPECTATOR)

FRUSTRATION.

Disappointment; defeat; a grating chagrin born
of thwarted hopes, and often associated with
the coming of Brexit.

'*smites their most refined policies with frustration and
a curse*' (SOUTH)

'*This Brexit was born of frustration and so 'twill bring
more in its train.*' (WEST)

FUMBLE.

To manage awkwardly, oft-times used of our current managing of Brexit.

'He fumbles up all' (SHAKESPEARE)

'They fumble up Brexit'
(SHAKESPEARE, UNTOWARD FOLIO)

FUSCATION.

The act of darkening or obscuring. So, *foxation*, a cunning act of obscuring one's own tracks. Also *forfucksation*, resigned feeling among Remainers.

GERMAN. (1)

Brother.

'their cousin german' (SPENSER)

Of a brother nation to Britain.

'our German cousin' (MARX)

GERMAN. (2)

Related; closely related to the British. Obsolete.

'those that are german' (SHAKESPEARE)

'them that are German'
(SHAKESPEARE, DOUBTFUL QUARTO)

GLACIOUS.

Icy; resembling ice; appearing elegant and polite but inwardly chill; a regal or diplomatic manner.

'Good Mistress May did greet the French and Hispanic Ambassadors in her most glacious manner.'
(PRETTY-SWIFT)

HAMMER.

The instrument consisting of a long handle and heavy head, with which anything is forged or driven.

Anything destructive.

So, *Hammond*, an instrument consisting of a long face and heavy heart, thought to be destructive of Brexit.

HARD (BREXIT).

Firm; resisting penetration or separation; not soft. Hence much used of a type of Brexit that is firm, resisting explanation or negotiation; not soft.

'While I to the hard house
More hard than is the stone whereof 'tis rais'd'
(SHAKESPEARE, KING LEAR)

'Prithee Nuncle Boris, why is thy boiled egg like unto a Brexit? Nay, 'tis a hard riddle to crack'
(FESTE TO SIR BORIS, IN
SHAKESPEARE, THIRTEENTH NIGHT)

HATCHET FACE.

A face such, one supposes, as might be hewn out of a block by a hatchet. Hence also, by extension, **BREXIT FACE**, an expression such as might be hewn out of a block by a Brexit. So, *Brexit-faced*, having such an expression.

'On the night of the referendum, both the Remain and the Leave leaders were Brexit-faced.'

HEDGE (FUND).

Hedge prefixed to any word denotes something mean, vile or of the lowest class.

'the hedge-priest'   (SHAKESPEARE)

'the hedge fund'   (SHAKESPEARE, IMPOVERISHED FOLIO)

'Though the government funds may subside, the wretched hedge funds will flourish still.'
                              (ADDIDSON ON THE SOUTH-SEA BREXIT)

HOP (OFF).

A jump; a light leap; the mode of progression of the frog. Hence *to hop off*, to depart in the manner of the frog from a lily pad. Much used as an expression in tirades, witty or otherwise, on Britain's neighbours with nostalgic reference to ancient wars.

'Ah I have seen the time I did make the French hop off; Pass me some sack, sirrah innkeeper!'

                              (MASTER NIGEL SHALLOW,
                        IN SHAKESPEARE, HENRY IV PART V,
                        OR HENRY V PART IV, WEIRD FOLIO)

HOUR (FINEST).

The twenty-fourth part of a natural day; a particular time; the zenith for some nostalgic spirits of Britain to which Brexit shall return us.

'their finest hour'   (CHURCHILL)

'our finest hour'
(SIR BORIS, IN SHAKESPEARE, HENRY V PART VI)

'my finest hour'
(MASTER NIGEL SHALLOW, IN SHAKESPEARE,
HENRY VIII PART VII)

HUFF.

[from *hove* or *hoven*] Swell of sudden anger or arrogance; a wretch swelled with a false opinion of his own value, as many find is the case of our current orators. Hence *to be in a huff* is then to be in a ferment, as we now speak.

Huffer-up is one who tries to make others get into a huff, as 'Sir Boris de Johnson was the supremely gifted huffer-up of his era in this country, as Master Trump was in America.'

HYGGEROMETER.

From *hygrometer*, instrument used to measure the degrees of moisture. Hence instrument used to measure the degrees of *hygge* or Danish-style cosiness or, by extension, general fashionable cant favoured by those in the know, or so they think. This hygge is said by some to be a consolation in time of Brexit.

IMPACT.

[*impactus*, Latin] To drive close or hard; to knock flat, over or down. Hence to be impacted by Brexit.

'being impacted so thick and confusedly together'
(WOODWARD)

'being impacted so thick and confusedly by Brexit'
(WOEDWARD)

'the œconomy is foretold to be entirely and utterly impacted by Brexit'

(HAMMOND'S ŒCONOMICAL FORECASTINGS)

So, *impact assessment*, a confused attempt to measure the impact of Brexit, both promised and withheld, at the same time insanely detailed and non-existent.

INDEPENDENCE.

Freedom; exemption from reliance or control; state over which no one has power. State of wild or oblivious uproar, as in 'United Kingdom Independence Party'.

'Let fortune do her worst, whatever she makes us lose, as long as she never makes us lose our honesty and our independence.'   (POPE)

'Let Mistress May do her worst, and empty all the coffers of the kingdom, as long as she never makes us lose our honesty and our independence.'

(MASTER NIGEL SHALLOW SPEAKING
TO HIS SUPPORTERS ON 'INDEPENDENCE DAY')

INFLUX.

Act of flowing into anything; unwelcoming view taken by Brexit-oriented orators of those seeking to live in a country.

INSURRECTION.

A seditious rising; a rebellious commotion; a populist uprising such as some have discerned in Brexit.

*'Like to a little kingdom, suffers then
The nature of an insurrection.'* (SHAKESPEARE)

*'Like as this United Kingdom did suffer then
The nature of an insurrection.'*

(SHAKESPEARE, THE TRAGICAL
HISTORIE AND DELECTABLE COMEDIE
OF BREXIT, MOULDY FOLIO)

INWALL.

To inclose or fortify with a wall.
    Inwaller. One who attempts to wall in.
    Inwalled. Condition of having been fortified by a wall, as 'Mr Trump assured them they had been inwalled for their own protection.'

IRE.

[French; from *ira*, Latin] Anger; rage; passionate hatred.
    So, *ireful*, angry; raging; furious.

'In midst of all the dome misfortune sat,
And gloomy discontent, and fell debate,
And madness laughing in his ireful mood.' (DRYDEN)

And *Ireland*, a passionate country oft driven
to anger, rage and hatred by the actions of its
neighbour.

IRRECOVERABLY.

Beyond recovery; past repair.

'O dark, dark, dark amid' the blaze of noon;
Irrecoverably dark, total eclipse,
Without all hope of day.'

(MILTON'S SAMSON AGONISTES)

'The credit of the exchequer is irrecoverably lost by the
last breach with the bankers.'   (TEMPLE)

'The credit of the Greek exchequer is irrecoverably lost
by the last breach with the European Central Bank.'
(PSEUDO-VAROUFAKIS)

'The credit of the British exchequer was irrecoverably lost
when Britain plunged out of the European Exchange
Rate Mechanism.'   (SIR GORDON BROWNE)

KAW.

The cry of a raven or crow.

Hence *kaw-kaw*, long cry of a single crow or cries of pairs of crows.

KICKSHAW.

A dish so changed by the cooking that it can scarcely be known.

So, **BREXSHAW** (sometimes, coarsely, Brexshit), an enterprise so changed by negotiation that it can scarcely be recognized.

'I am but mad north-north-west; when the wind is southerly I can tell a Björk from a Brexshaw.'
(SHAKESPEARE, HAMLET, VERY BAD QUARTO)

KITTEN.

To bring forth young cats.

'Brexit makes us kitten.'   (ADDIDSON AND STEAL)

LEADSOM.

Leadman, one who begins or leads a dance. So, *Leadsom*, one capable of leading a portion of a party a merry dance, though apt to break off abruptly.

'You can mis-Leadsom of the people all of the time, and all of the people some of the time, but not all of the people all of the time.'   (PROVERB)

LEAP-FROG.

A play of children in which they imitate the jump of frogs.

'If I could win a lady at leap-frog.'
(SHAKESPEARE, HENRY V)

'If I could win a trade deal at leap-frog.'
(DAFFIDAVIS, IN THE DAILY DEPRESSED)

An attempt to jump over an obstacle or a rival, often used of Britain and Europe, as 'Brits to leap-frog the frogs' (*Ye Bright Sonne*).

LEXICOGRAPHER.

A writer of dictionaries; a harmless drudge who busies himself or herself in tracing the original, and detailing the signification of words.

Hence also **BREXICOGRAPHER**, a writer of Brexit dictionaries, a harmless drudge who busies himself or herself in tracing the original and current insignification of words.

LINE (RED).

Longitudinal extension; slender string. Hence *red line*, extremely slender, longitudinal extension or string, painted bright red in a vain attempt to make it appear less slender and more longitudinal. Hence any notional limit, generally ignored in proportion to the extravagance of the threats associated with crossing it.

'A line seldom holds to strain.' (MOXON)

'A red line seldom holds to strain.' (FOXON)

LION.

The fiercest and most magnanimous of four-footed beasts. The fiercest and most ranting of phrases in much Brexiteer discourse.

'See lion-hearted Richard
Piously valiant' (PHILIPS)

'Let the nation once more roar like the olden-time lion.'
(SIR BORIS)

LOON, LOONY.

Loon, a sorry fellow; a scoundrel; a rascal. Hence *loony*, acting most like a sorry fellow or scoundrel or rascal, and hence in recent controversies used of one who disagrees with the speaker on a matter of importance.

'European Union denounces most loony Brexiteers.'
(ADDIDSON)

'Brexiteers denounce most loony European Union.'
(ADDIDSON)

'European Loony-on' (YE BRIGHT SONNE)

LOSER.

A person who is deprived of anything; one who forfeits anything; the contrary to winner or gainer; a popular and widespread term of indiscriminate belittlement, generally these days used as a plural.

'losers and malcontents' (SOUTH)

''Twas losers and malcontents did vote for Brexit.'
(FARTHER SOUTH)

''Tis losers and malcontents who do obstruct Brexit.'
(NORTH)

Bad loser, one who defeated President Trump in the popular vote.

LOTTERY.

A game of chance; a sortilege; distribution of prizes by chance. A play in which lots are drawn for prizes; delusive prospect of vast wealth; main source of hope that one will be immune to the economic consequences of Brexit.

LOZENGE.

A form of medicine made into small pieces to be held or chewed in the mouth until melted or wasted, especially when making speeches. Antidote to throttling of Brexit pronouncements.

LUMBER, LUMBERED.

From lumber, to heap like useless goods irregularly. Hence *lumbered*, to be burdened by an irregular and useless heap of stuff, as 'lumbered with Brexit', 'lumbered with Boris', 'lumbered with Trump'.

MACHINATION (CASH).

[*machinatio*, Latin; *machination*, French]
Artifice; contrivance; malicious scheme. Hence
cash machination, an artifice or malicious
scheme for using or deploying cash.

*'The cash machinations of the great banks are
ubiquitous.'*

(ADAM SMYTH)

MAFFLE.

To stammer. Hence *maffled*, hesitant, as

'Be not maffled – have thou this magic lozenge.'
(Chancellor Sweet to Good Mistress May,
in Shakespeare, dodgy quarto)

MALCONTENT or
MALECONTENT.

One who is dissatisfied; one whom nothing pleases.

'Here comes now the malcontent, a singular fellow, and very formall in all his demeanours; one that can reprove the world with but a word, the follies of the people with a shrug!' (Riche)

'Eleven self-consumed malcontents pull the rug from under our EU negotiators.' (Ye Daily Chain Mail)

'Nothing seemed to please the malcontent Brexiteers.'
(Addison)

MARMALADE.

A quince, Portuguese. Traditional British accompaniment of toast and butter.

'Marmalade is the pulp of quinces boiled into a consistence with sugar; it is subastringent, grateful to the stomach.' (QUINCY)

'Marmalade is the quintessence of British breakfast-time.' (MARTIN DE QUINCEY)

MAY.

To be possible.

'Politics is the Art of May be' (ADDIDSON)

Hence also to be by chance.

'It may be' (SHAKESPEARE)

'It may be May (for a bit longer).'
(SHAKESPEARE, THE HARD WINTER'S TALE)

MÉNAGE.

A collection of animals.

'I saw here the largest ménage that I ever met with.'
(ADDISON)

So, *ménage à trois, -quatre, -cinq*, a collection of animals rumoured to be found in the leading hotels of Muscovy.

MERCER.

One who sells silks. Thus one who sells fabrics generally. So also one who sells and purveys through divers channels fabricated stuffs of all kinds.

METROPOLIS.

The chief city of any country or district. A place of enviable extravagance with ornate and expensive streets and a wildly inflated housing market where none can afford to live but millionaires; a situation supposed by some to be put to rights by Brexit, which though others do sorely doubt.

'or some renown'd metropolis,
With glist'ring spires and pinnacles adorn'd.'

(MILTON)

'For Sale in the heart of the Metropolis. Five-bedroom
house with glist'ring spires and pinnacles, £5,000,000'
(MILTON'S ESTATE AGENTS, LONDON)

MILLION.

The number of an hundred myriads, or ten hundred thousand. A proverbial name for any very great number.

To million, to speak vaguely of many millions in the course of an argument or discourse, and much resorted to in our more technical and financial Brexit passages, as

'*Sir Boris was apt at millioning about the advantages of leaving the EU.*'

MINATORY.

[*minor*, Latin] Threatening.

'*The king made a statute monitory and minatory, towards justices of the peace, that they should duly execute their office, inviting complaints against them.*'

(BACON, HENRY VII)

'*Ye Daily Chain Mail made minatory headlines towards the justices who had determined that Parliament must have the final say on Brexit, inviting complaints against them. Thereafter Mistress May determined to make use of the minatory Henry VIII powers, circumventing Parliament altogether.*'

(BACKON, HENRY VIII REDUX)

MIND-BOGGLER, MIND-BOGGLING.

From *boggler*, a doubter, a timorous man. Hence a *mind-boggler*, one who renders the mind full of doubts or astonishment; *mind-boggling*, that which boggles the mind, as all sides of our current dispute may often do.

'The Remain campaign was full of mind-boggling detail.'　　　　　　　　　(Addidson)

'The Brexit campaign showed a mind-boggling absence of detail.'　　　　　　(Addidson)

MOAN.

To lament, to deplore; to make lamentation.

'where misery moans'　　　　　　　(Thomson)

Hence *remoan*, to relament, to redeplore; to remake lamentation for Brexit.

'where misery remoans'　　　　(Thomson Twins)

And also *remoaner*, term used dismissively of one who has any shade of doubt about Brexit, as

'Remoaners moan on about Brexit triumph!'
　　　　　　　　　　　(Daily Chain Mail)

MONSIEUR.

A term of reproach for a Frenchman, as 'Non mais alors, Monsieur Davis!'　　　(M. Barnier)

MUDDLE.

To make turbid, to make half-drunk, hence a *muddle*, something turbid or as if seen when half-drunk, as 'this Brexit muddle', and *muddled*, talking or acting as if half-drunk, as

'I was for five years often drunk, always muddled.'
(ARBUTHNOT, THE HISTORY OF JOHN BULL)

'Everyone concerned seemed somewhat muddled when they attempted to expound the Brexit policies.'
(ADDIDSON)

MULETEER.

Mule-driver, hence by analogy, **BREXITEER**, Brexit-driver.

MUSKETEER.

A soldier whose weapon is his musket, and hence by analogy, **BREXITEER**, a politician whose main weapon is his Brexit.

MUSTY.

Mouldy; endlessly repeating the word *must*, as 'we must leave', 'I must be off'.

'And this is Mr Daffidavis, my most musty lieutenant.'
(GOOD MISTRESS MAY, IN SHAKESPEARE,
HENRY IV PART IV, SCENE AT YE TABARD,
ONLY IN THE FOOLISH FOLIO)

MUTINEER.

A mover of sedition; a mover of seditious parliamentary amendments to Brexit bills; an opposer of lawful authority; an opposer of Brexit authority.

'They have cashiered several of their opponents as mutineers, who have contradicted them in political conversations.' (ADDISON)

'They have cashiered several of their opponents as mutineers, who have contradicted them in Brexit conversations.' (ADDIDSON)

MUTTONFIST.

[from *mutton* and *fist*] A hand large and red. Hence also *muttonfisted*, handling clumsily.

'The handling of EU agricultural policy was extremely muttonfisted.' (ADDISON)

MUZZLE.

To bind the mouth.

'My dagger muzzled
Lest it should bite its master, and so prove,
As ornaments oft do, too dangerous.'

(SHAKESPEARE, THE WINTER'S TALE)

'I have the government muzzled, lest it should bite its
master.'   (SIR MURDO MURDOCH)

Also to fondle with the mouth close. A low word.

'They did exchange many a muzzling message.'
(BOOKE OF REBEKAH AND DAVID,
APOCRYPHA)

MYOLOGY.

The description and doctrine of the muscles;
the attempt to grab hold using the muscles of
as much as possible of the world.

'Sir Boris was fast becoming one of the heroes of our
national myology.'   (QUITE-SWIFT)

MYTHOLOGY.

System of fables; explication of the fabulous
history of the gods of the heathen world.

'The modesty of mythology deserves to be commended:
the scenes there are laid at a distance; it is once

*upon a time, in the days of yore, and in the land
of Utopia.'*

(BENTLEY)

Less modestly, equivalent to *fake news*, a system
of fables; explication of the fabulous history of
EU regulation.

NATIVE.

A person born in any place; original inhabitant; one disinclined to travel; much revived as a favourable term by those of Brexit-inclined views.

'the lowly natives of a country town' (DRYDEN)

'the Brexit natives of a country town' (DRYPEN)

'The natives are getting Brexit.'
  (THE DAILY DEPRESSED)

NEGOTIATOR.

A person employed to treat with others; and often across many centuries, those employed to treat with Europe for Britain.

'Those who have defended the proceedings of our negoti-ators at Gertruydenburg, dwell much upon their zeal in endeavouring to work the French up to their demands; but say nothing to justify those demands.' (SWIFT)

'Those defending the zeal of our Brexit negotiators dwell more on their ability to work the French up than on their skill in negotiation.' (THE LESS-SWIFT)

NEWS.

Fresh account of anything; something not heard before. Almost solely concerned with Brexit in recent times, though whether much of that is unheard before is doubtful. Some also fear that for news we do substitute mere sentiment and opinion.

'Their papers, filled with a different party spirit, divide the people into different sentiments, who generally consider rather the principles than the truth of the news-writer.' (ADDISON)

'Their Facebook pages and Twitter feeds, filled with a different party spirit, divide the people into different

Brexit and anti-Brexit sentiments, who generally consider rather the principles than the truth of the news-sources.'
                                                    (ADDIDSON)

NO (DEAL).

[*na*, Saxon] The word of refusal, contrary to *yea* or *yes*. Regarded by many as the bone of contention in these Brexit turmoils.

'Oh sir, we do say a hearty yes to no
and a full-throated no to yea.'

                    (SIR BORIS, IN SHAKESPEARE, CONFUSING FOLIO)

'No deal means non deal, no means non.'
            (COMMISSIONER BARMIER, IN LE FUNNY OLD MONDE)

NOTIFICATION.

Act of making known, as 'European Union (Notification of Withdrawal) Act 2017'.

NUTJOBBER.

A bird. Also an emissary of Sir Rolling Dacres, sent to quieten Remainers.

OAF.

[Variously written *auff*, *ofe* and *oph*; it seems a corruption of *ouph*, a demon or fairy, in German *alf*, from which *elf*: and means properly the same with *changeling*, a foolish child left by malevolent *ouphs* or *fairies*, in the place of one more witty, which they steal away.] A dolt; a blockhead; an idiot.

Hence also **BROAF** (also written *Br-off*), one on the British side who tries to force Brexit through with bluster and menace, and without dialogue, and equally *EUff* (also written *Eu-off*), one on the European Union team who tries to prevent Brexit by bluster and threat, and without dialogue.

'Who has ta'en my ministers and left me these Broaffs in their place?'

(GOOD QUEEN MAY, IN SHAKESPEARE,
A MIDWINTER'S NIGHT'S DREAM, LOST QUARTO)

*'Thou'rt no good elf but a mischievous Euff,
Therefore Puck thee off into yon wood'*

(ROCKY BOTTOM, IN SHAKESPEARE,
A MIDWINTER'S NIGHT'S DREAM, IMPERFECT QUARTO)

OATS.

A grain which in England is generally given to horses, but in Scotland supports the people.

So, **BROATS**, a kind of coarse grain on which Britons will subsist after Brexit.

OFFICIAL.

An official person.

'Official is that person to whom the cognisance of causes is committed by such as have ecclesiastical jurisdiction.'

(AYCLIFFE)

Hence a *Euro official*, one on whom all British ills may be conveniently blamed.

'Official is that person to whom the cognisance of causes is committed by such as have Euro jurisdiction. Generally called Barmier.'　(BEECLIFFE)

OLIGARCHY, OLIGARCH.

A form of government which places the supreme power in a small number; much feared as both cause and consequence of Brexit by some around town.

'The worst kind of oligarchy is, when men are governed indeed by a few, and yet are not taught to know what those few be, whom they should obey.'　(SIDNEY)

'All oligarchies, wherein a few men domineer, do what they list.'　(YE DAILY CHAIN MAIL)

Hence *oligarch*, one of small number who wield supreme power.

'Oligarch? Me?'　(ARRANT BANKS)

Hence also an *oligarcharch*, building erected by an oligarch in tasteless or over-ornate style.

'Chelsea's new stadium will feature a vast and imposing oligarcharcharch.' (THE DAILY DEPRESSED)

And also *arch-oligarch*, the supreme oligarch of an oligarchy.

'Mr Puton is said to be arch-oligarch of all Muscovy.' (ADDIDSON)

ONSET.

Attack; storm; first brunt.

*'The shout
Of battle now began, and rushing sound
Of onset.'* (MILTON, PARADISE LOST)

*'The shout
Of Brexit now began, and rushing round
Of onset.'* (MILTON, PARADISE MISLAID)

OPTIMITY.

[from *optimus*, Latin] The state of being best. Hence also *proxoptimity*, the state of being nearly best and **BREXOPTIMITY**, the state of making the best of Brexit.

ORDERLY.

Methodical; regular; not tumultuous; lacking in unpleasant surprises.

'an orderly and well-governed march'   (CLARENDON)

'An orderly Brexit: why that's to say
A flame of ice, good madam: a thing
Much desired but little found'

(THE FOOL, IN SHAKESPEARE,
FOURTEENTH NIGHT, ODD QUARTO)

PARLIAMENT-LUBBER.

From *abbey-lubber*, a slothful loiterer in a religious house, under pretence of retirement and austerity. So, *parliament-lubber*, a slothful loiterer in the Houses of Parliament or in the European Parliament, under pretence of being an active legislator, desirous of obtaining a pension while attempting to undermine the institution.

PATRIOT, PATRIOTISM.

A person whose ruling passion is love of his or her country. Sometimes used for a factious disturber of the government, notably even from within itself in our troubled times.

'Patriotism is the last refuge of a scoundrel.'
                    (S. JOHNSON AS REPORTED BY BOSWELL)

'Thou'rt a great Patriot, Sir Boris, very great,
But on mine honour I am a bigger one.
Pass the ale, bully landlord!'

(MASTER NIGEL SHALLOW,
IN SHAKESPEARE HENRY IV PART II,
TERRIBLE ACTOR'S FOLIO)

PHONOCAMPTICK.

Having the power to inflect and turn the sound, and latterly, by extension, employing or speaking with the very loud and heightened manner of speech most commonly adopted when talking into a mobile phone device. Hence, by extension, using the voice or tone associated with the mobile phone in general or publick discourse.

'Our politicians speak increasingly in phonocamptick tones.'   (ADDIDSON)

POST (-TRUTH).

A hasty messenger; a courier who comes and goes at stated times; hence *post-truth*, a hastily contrived 'truth', a truth which comes and goes at stated times.

'In certain places there be always fresh posts to carry that farther which is brought unto them.'

(ADDISON)

'In certain places, there be always fresh post-truths to carry that farther which is brought unto them.'

(ADDIDSON)

PRETERPLUPERFECT.

A grammatical term applied to the tense that denotes time absolutely past. Hence **BREXPLUPERFECT**, a grammatical term applied to the tense that denotes time idealised by Brexiteers but absolutely in the past.

PROFLUENT.

Flowing forwards. Hence professionally flowing on and on.

'the profluent stream'

(MILTON)

'Thou art the most profluent, Sir Boris,
But I am the more effluent.'

(MASTER NIGEL SHALLOW,
IN SHAKESPEARE, HENRY VIIIb)

PUMP(S) (ALL HANDS TO).

An engine by which water is drawn up from
wells; a safety device for use in a rising flood,
usually plural and rarely effective it would
appear, but much invoked in the emergencies
of Brexit.

'All hands to the pumps, once more unto the Brexit,
don't panic!'

(GOOD KING HAL, IN SHAKESPEARE,
HENRY V PART Ic, POOR FOLIO)

QUACK.

[*quacken*, Dutch, to cry as a goose] To cry like a duck, often written *quaake* to represent the sound better.

'Good my Lord Cameron Quaake, up before all is lost!'
(CHANCELLOR GEORGE FROGSPAWN,
IN THOMAS MIDDLESBROUGH,
THE REFERENDER'S TRAGEDY)

QUIBBLE.

A slight cavil, notably with less slight consequences in technical and Brexical controversy.

'Having once fully answered your quibble, you will not, I hope, expect that I should do it again and again.'

(WATERLAND)

'Having once fully answered your quibble, you will, of course, expect that I should do it again and again, n'est-ce pas?'

(OVERHEARD REMARK BY M. BARMIER TO MR DAFFIDAVIS IN THE COURSE OF THE BREXIT NEGOTIATIONS)

Hence *to quibble*, to slightly cavil at, as

'Dost thou quibble at me, Monsieur?'

(SIR BORIS, IN SHAKESPEARE, HENRY V PART VIII, QUIRKY QUARTO)

QUITRENT.

Small rent reserved; not so small rent payable to depart from a European Union or price of Brexit.

'a small quitrent, which everyone would be content to pay'

(TEMPLE)

*'a huge, immense, vast quitrent for Brexit which no one
would be content to pay'*   (YE DAILY CHAIN MAIL)

QUOTA.

A share; a proportion as assigned to each,
whether of soldiery or of commodities. A
requirement and at the same time a limit much
derided and feared by Brexiteers.

*'Scarce one in this list but engages to supply a quota
of brisk young fellows, equipt with hats and feathers.'*
(ADDISON)

*'We say fishing and you say quota; we say exports and
you say quota; we say apples and you say quota – let's
call the whole thing off.'*

(REMARKS OF MR DAFFIDAVIS TO
M. BARMIER, AS OVERHEARD AND
REPORTED BY THE DAILY DEPRESSED)

RAWHEAD.

The name of a spectre, mentioned to fright children.

'Hence draw thy theme, and to the stage permit
Rawhead and bloody bones, and hands and feet,
Ragousts for Tereus or Thyestes drest.'   (DRYDEN)

The spectre of a suffering person fleeing perse-cution, in a large crowd, summoned to fright voters.

REASONABLE.

Having the faculty of reason; endued with reason; acting, speaking or thinking rationally. Hence often used of the British, and equally of the Conservative faction as being the most entirely British faction in our political realm.

'such forces as were held sufficient to hold in bridle either the malice or rage of reasonable people' (HAYWARD)

'such Brexit as was held sufficient to hold in bridle either the malice or rage of reasonable people' (WAYWARD)

REFERENDARY.

[*referendus*, Latin] One to whose decision anything is referred, and thus also one who refers everything back to the Brexit referendum result, despite its being ambiguous and receding ever farther into the distance, as

'The news-sheets generally took a referendary approach to every new question that arose.' (QUITE-SWIFT)

REGLEMENT.

[French] Regulation. A rather Gallic word. Not used.

'the reformation and reglement'   (BACON)

'We must have bon reglement of Brexit.'   (BARMIER)

REGRET.

[*regret*, French; *regretto*, Italian] Vexation at something past; bitterness of vexation, much denied on all sides of the current Brexit controversy.

'Je ne regret nothing.'
                    (M. BARMIER ON HIS CONDUCT
                    OF THE BREXIT NEGOTIATIONS)

'Regret? Nyet.'   (PSEUDO-PUTIN)

REGULATION.

The act of regulating; method; the effect of being regulated.

'They cannot continue any regular and constant motion, without the guidance and regulation of some intelligent being.'   (JOHN RAY)

Hence much brandished of Brexit, *deregulation*, the act of deregulating, randomness, the effect of being deregulated, whether desirable or doubtful.

'The market will cease any regular and constant motion, through lack of guidance and deregulation.'

(LORD CANNY, YE BANKE OF ENGLAND)

REGULATOR.

A person who regulates; that part of a machine which makes the motion equitable. Hence *regulatory*, of that part of a machine which makes the motion equitable, and *regulatory alignment*, the way a machine is kept equable by its regulator.

'When there is no regulatory alignment in the engine of state, the wheels do fall off on all sides.' (ADDIDSON)

REMAIN.

To be left out of a greater quantity or number, as, for example, 48% is left out of 100%. To remain is also to continue in a place, as to continue in Europe. Hence also a *Remainer*, one who belongs to 48% out of 100% and continues, or would continue, in Europe.

RESENTMENT.

[*ressentiment*, French] Deep sense of injury; anger long continued, sometimes simply anger. Also *to resent*, as all sides increasingly do. An infectious passion.

'On behalf of the French republic and its people, I resent your last remark about les grenouilles, Monsieur Daffidavis.'   (M. Barnier/Barmier)

RESIDENTIARY.

[from *resident*] Holding residence.

'Christ was the conductor of the Israelites into the land of Canaan, and their residentiary guardian.'
(Thomas More)

'Where is the residentiary guardian of our guests from Europe?'
(Thomas More, Lost Letters to Erasmus)

'Christ was the conductor of the Europeans into the land of Britain, and is ever still their residentiary guardian against our neglect.'
(Thomas More, More Lost Letters to Erasmus)

RUDDOCK.

[*rubecula*, Latin] A kind of bird.

'Of singing birds, they have linnets, and ruddocks.'
(Carew)

So, *Rudd[ock]*, a bird that sings more sweetly than the coughing Mayfowl.

RUMINATE.

To chew over again; to muse on; to meditate over and over again.

'The condemn'd English
Sit patiently, and inly ruminate.'   (SHAKESPEARE)

Hence also *remainate*, to meditate over and over again on the desire to remain in Europe and thus not to Brexit.

'The depress'd Remainers
Sit patiently, and inly remainate.'

(SHAKESPEARE, DODGY QUARTO)

SCOTCH.

To put paid to, partially.

'We have scotch'd the snake, not kill'd it.'
(SHAKESPEARE, MACBETH)

'We have scotch'd the Brexit, not kill'd it.'
(THE LADY STURGEON OF NESS)

SHAMBLING.

Moving awkwardly and irregularly; inclining towards the *shambolic*. A low bad word but found apt by many to describe certain characters.

'By that shambling in his walk, it should be my rich banker.'
(DRYDEN)

'By that shambling in his walk, it should be my rich steward or rather the Foreign Secretary.'
(MISTRESS MAY, IN SHAKESPEARE,
THIRTEENTH NIGHT, BLURRED QUARTO)

SKEWER.

A wooden or iron pin, used to keep meat in form. Hence *to skewer*, to fasten with skewers, and also to fasten an argument or person in debate with skewers.

'Bold Daffidavis skewers Monskewer Barmier!'
(YE BRIGHT SONNE)

SLAVER.

Spittle running from the mouth; drivel. So, **BREX-SLAVER**, drivel running from the mouths of Brexiteers and the presses of Brexit-supporting newspapers.

SOFT (BREXIT).

Not hard, not rugged, not rough; oft-times used of a type of Brexit that is not hard, not rugged, not rough, and in the hopes of some who speak so, not catastrophic.

'Some bodies are hard, and some soft; the hardness is caused by the jejuneness of the spirits, which, if in a greater degree, make them not only hard, but fragil.'

(BACON)

'Some Brexits are hard, and some soft; the hardness is caused by the jejuneness of the negotiators, which, if in a greater degree, make them not only hard but fragil.'

(RASHER)

SOP.

Anything steeped in liquor, commonly to be eaten; anything given to pacify, from the sop given to Cerberus to that given to inflamed British negotiators.

'The prudent Sibyl had before prepar'd
A sop, in honey steep'd, to charm the guard.'

(DRYDEN)

'The prudent Barmier had before prepar'd
A sop, with honey'd words, to charm the Brits.'

(DRYPEN)

SOVEREIGNTY.

Supremacy; highest place; supreme power; highest degree of excellence; the supposed goal and bone of contention in Brexit.

'your unknown sovereignty'
(SHAKESPEARE, MEASURE FOR MEASURE)

'Your sovereignty? I know nothing of your sovereignty.'
(MONSIEUR BARMIER
SUMMARIZED IN YE DAILY CHAIN MAIL)

STABLE.

Fixed, able to stand; fixed in a state or condition; much favoured as a term of political virtue by Good Mistress May and her ministers.

'He perfect, stable; but imperfect we'
(DRYDEN'S CHAUCER)

'The table appeared stable, but this appearance was but till they put a small plate thereon – and thus it was with the prime minister too.'
(SMULLETT)

'I command the waves to stand stable.'   (KING CNUT)

STANDARD(S).

That which is of undoubted authority; that which is the test of other things of the same kind; that which it is much feared will fall as a result of Brexit.

'Our measures of length I cannot call standards, for standard measures must be certain and fixed.'
(HOLDER)

'Our measures of food safety I cannot call standards, for standards must be certain and fixed.' (MOULDER)

STRONG.

Vigorous, forceful, of great ability of body.

'that our oxen may be strong to labour'
(PSALM CXLIV.14)

'that our oxen may be strong and stable'
(SLOGAN CXV.17)

STURGEON.

[*sturio, tursio*, Latin] A sea-fish of enormous size and imposing anatomy, as 'It is part of a scutellated bone of a sturgeon' (Woodward). It is said to originate in the Caspian Sea, and from its roe caviare is made. So, a large fish in a small pond.

'The SNP policy on Brexit was caviare to the general.'
(SHAKESPEARE, HAMLET, DODGY FOLIO)

SUCCESSFUL.

Prosperous; happy; fortunate.

'They were terrible alarms to persons grown wealthy by a long and successful imposture, by persuading the world that men might be honest and happy, though they never mortified any corrupt appetites.'

(SOUTH)

'We will achieve a successful Brexit by mortifying the entire œconomy.'

(MISTRESS MAY)

SURCHARGE.

Burthen added to burthen; more than can be well borne. Charge put sur British goods or people by Europe as a result of Brexit.

'a surcharge of one madness upon another'

(L'ESTRANGE)

'a madness of one Euro surcharge on top of another'

(YE DAILY CHAIN MAIL)

SURE.

Certainly, without doubt, doubtless.

'Something sure of state…
Hath puddled his clear spirit.'

(SHAKESPEARE, OTHELLO)

'*Something sure of Brexit*
Doth puddle Mistress May's clear spirit.'

(SHAKESPEARE, MOTHELLO, DOUBTFUL QUARTO)

Hence also *oh sure*, as

'*Does Brexit proceed apace, Master Daffidavis?*' '*Oh*
sure, it doth, Mistress May.'

(SHAKESPEARE,

A MIDSUMMER NIGHT'S BREXIT,

VERY DOUBTFUL FOLIO)

TAKE (BACK).

To fasten on, to seize.

'Wheresoever he taketh him he teareth him: and he foameth.' (MARK IX.18)

Hence *to take back*, to seize once more, and *to take back control*, to seize control once more, as many say is the true essential motive for Brexit.

'Wheresoever we taketh back control, we shall tear about, and we shall foam too.' (Boris xxx.99)

'Wheresoever we have ta'en back control, we shall swear't, and we shall foam with good ale and we want to know who shall stop us?' (Nigel xvi.199)

TALK.

Oral conversation; fluent and familiar speech; in plural, *talks*, infinitely ongoing oral conversations to resolve Brexit deal.

'And whose talk is of bullocks?'
(Ecclesiastes xxxviii.25)

'And are these Brexit talks not full of bullocks?'
(Ye Daily Chain Mail)

'much talk and little knowledge' (Locke)

'much Brexit talks and little knowledge' (Lock)

TANK (THINK).

A large cistern or bason. Hence a *think tank*, a large cistern or bason-full of ideas.

'Before joining the Ministry of Environment as special advisor, he worked for the Climate-Change denial think tank Fossil Lies.'

TEA.

A Chinese plant, of which the infusion has lately been much drunk in Europe; in its strong and milky form, a distinctly British habit. Claimed by some as an emblem of Brexit Britain.

'I have filled a teapot, and received a dish of it.'

(ADDISON)

'Tea is in the middle of the very name of Britain.'

(ADDIDSON)

'Du thé, Monsieur Daffidavis?'

(TABLE TALK OF M. BARMIER)

TERM(S).

Condition, stipulation, notably for a smooth departure from Europe.

'Well, on my terms, thou wilt not be my heir.'

(DRYDEN)

'Well, on my terms, thou wilt not be mein Herr.'

(FRAU MERKEL'S VIEW OF EU NEGOTIATIONS
AS REPORTED IN YE DAILY CHAIN MAIL)

TÊTE-À-TÊTE.

Cheek by jowl; intimate manner of conversing. In English, head-to-head or locking horns, as in the manner of conversing of Mr Davis and M. Barnier.

THATCHER.

A person whose trade is to cover houses with straw; one whose political trade is to cover up the Houses of Parliament with last straws.

'our thatcher' (SWIFT)

'our Thatcher' (NOT-SO-SWIFT)

Hence also proverbially, *thatcher's last straw*, the final straw in the covering of a house, as 'The treaty of Maastricht was Thatcher's last straw.' (Fairly-Swift)

TIME.

Measure of duration; a considerable space of duration, such as that employed in Brexiting.

'I have resolved to take time.' (SWIFT)

'I have resolved to waste time.'
(DAFFIDAVIS TO GOOD MISTRESS MAY)

'Alas, we are running out of time.'
(GOOD MISTRESS MAY TO DAFFIDAVIS)

'What's the time, good sirrah, for I know it not.'
(SIR BORIS TO MASTER NIGEL,
IN SHAKESPEARE, HENRY IV PART IV)

'Where have we put that timetable?'
(GOOD MISTRESS MAY TO SIR BORIS AND DAFFIDAVIS, IN
SHAKESPEARE, FOURTEENTH NIGHT, TERRIBLE QUARTO)

TRAITOR.

A person who being trusted betrays; one who disagrees in any way with Brexit.

There is no difference, in point of morality, whether a man calls me traitor in one word, or says I am one hired to betray my religion and sell my country,'
(SWIFT)

There is no difference, in point of morality, whether a troll calls me traitor in one word, or says I am one hired to betray Brexit and sell my country.'
(FAIRLY-SWIFT-TOO)

TRANSITION.

Removal; passage from one to another. Change; made of change. Hence often used of a liminal period during which Brexit becomes Brexit.

'a virtual transition'   (BACON'S NATURAL HISTORY)

'*a messy transition*' (BACKON'S BREXIT HISTORY)

'*an immediate transition*' (WOODWARD ON GEOLOGY)

'*a not-so-immediate transition*'
(WOODWARD ON BREXITOLOGY)

TROUL, TROLL.

[*trollen*, Dutch, to roll] To move volubly; to utter volubly; to utter *fake news* volubly.

'*Will you troul the catch?*'
(SHAKESPEARE, THE TEMPEST)

'*Will you catch the troul?*'
(SHAKESPEARE, THE BREXPEST)

Hence also *like a Russian troll*, referring to one troll inside another on Twitter.

TRUMP.

[*trompe*, Dutch and Old French] A trumpet; an instrument of warlike musick.

'*the wakeful trump of doom*' (MILTON)

'*the wakeful Trump of doom*' (RON MILTON)

TUMOROUS.

Swelling, protuberant. Vainly pompous; falsely magnificent, as

'Sir Boris's speech and appearance were not so much humorous as tumorous.'

'The Guard of Honour at the Elysée Palace appeared tumorous to British eyes, accustomed only to the modest Changing of the Guard at Buckingham Palace.'

TURKEY.

[*gallina turcica*, Latin] A large domestick fowl, supposed to be brought from Turkey. A large country not in the EU.

So, *young turk[ey]*, a large domestick politician, of partly Turkish origin, inclined to strut. So also *not-so-young turk[ey]*.

TUSK.

[*tasken*, Old Frisick] The long teeth of a pugnacious animal, the fang; the long president of a pugnacious Union.

'we must stick to our Tusk'

(Monsieur Barmier as reported in Le Funny Olde Monde)

TUSKED.

Furnished with tusks; stabbed by a tusk.

'The British negotiator argued that the talks had been tusked.' (ADDIDSON)

TWITTER.

Any motion or disorder of passion, such as a violent fit of laughing, or fit of fretting, as 'Mr Trump caused a great deal of global twitter.'

TWO (FINGERS).

One and one. Hence one finger and one finger.

'Let us raise two fingers in a victory salute!'
(THE DAILY DEPRESSED)

'By Brexit truly the populace hath raised two fingers to the world.' (BACKON)

ULTIMITY.

The last stage; the last consequence. A word very convenient, but not in use; a natural term for that fear or panic produced by the receipt of an ultimatum or final demand, as

'Daffidavis seemed to feel some ultimity after the ultimatum declared Britain had an hour to reach agreement on Brexit.'

UNACCEPTABLE.

Unpleasing; not such as is well received; not fitting in with Brexit and thus not to be contemplated.

'Tis as indecent as unacceptable.'
(GOVERNMENT OF THE TONGUE)

'The EU's haggling is as indecent as it is unacceptable.'
(TONGUE OF THE GOVERNMENT)

UNCONDITIONAL (SURRENDER).

Absolute, not limited by any terms. Hence *absolute surrender*, not limited by any terms. Hence also *to surrender unconditionally*, without limitation.

'We shall never surrender, well, not unconditionally, well, not absolutely unconditionally.'
(DAFFIDAVIS SPEECH AT BRUSSELS NEGOTIATIONS)

'Come out unconditionally with your hands up!'
(GERMAN MEP STATEMENT
AS REPORTED IN THE DAILY TELLOGRAPH)

UNDERHAND.

Secret; clandestine; sly; anti-Brexit.

'I had notice of my brother's purpose, and have by underhand means labour'd to dissuade him.'

(SHAKESPEARE, AS YOU LIKE IT)

'Labour had notice of the government's Brexit, and have by sneakily underhand means labour'd to prevent it.'

(SHAKESPEARE,
NOT QUITE AS YOU LIKE IT, TATTY QUARTO)

UNIVERSITY.

A school, where all the arts and faculties are taught and studied, and where, in the view of some news-sheets and politickal hacks, there are seditious lectures against Brexit.

UNWELCOME.

Not pleasing; not well received; not wanted round here, in the usage often associated with Brexit. Hence *feeling unwelcome*, feeling not well received nor wanted round here, and, by extension, *unwelcoming*, not pleased to see a visitor, not receiving a visitor or guest politely.

'Sunset-on-Sea: all visitors unwelcome!'

(BREXIT TOURIST BOARD CAMPAIGN)

VANCOURIER.

A harbinger; a precursor. So, *White-Vancourier*, an uncouth and speedy harbinger of Brexit, often marked by the flag of St George.

VEXATIOUS.

Afflictive, troublesome, causing trouble.

'Consider him maintaining his usurped title by continual vexatious wars against the kings of Judah.'   (SOUTH)

Hence also **BREXATIOUS**, afflictive, troublesome, causing trouble through Brexit, as

'Consider Daffidavis maintaining his fabricated title of Brexit Minister by continual Brexatious remarks against Monsieur Barmier.'

VIRELAY.

A sort of little ancient French poem, that consisted only of two rhymes and short verses, with stops. A somewhat prurient and sometimes rude video, that consists only of a few words and short snippets, which is most widely popular with the looser folk. Suspected by some of secretly inciting the passions of Brexiteers.

'if thou algate lust like virelays
And looser songs of love'   (Spenser)

VIRTUAL, VIRTUALLY.

Having the efficacy without the sensible or material part.

'virtual cold'   (Bacon)

'virtual or immediate touch?'   (Milton)

'virtual control' (PUTON)

Hence also *virtually*, in effect, though not materially.

'virtually contained' (HAMMOND'S FUNDAMENTALS)

'virtually bankrupt'
(HAMMOND'S FISCAL FUNDAMENTALS)

WAVERER.

A person unsettled and irresolute; one who cannot resolve to endorse Brexit wholeheartedly.

'Come, young waverer, come and go with me.'
(SHAKESPEARE)

'Come, young waverer, come and leave with me.'
(SHAKESPEARE, MISTY FOLIO)

'Madam, we are not wavering but drowning.'
(SYDNEY SMITH, BREXIT TABLE-TALK)

WEATHER.

State of the air respecting either cold or heat, wet or driness. The change of the state of the air. Tempest, storm.

'What's here, besides foul Brexit weather?'
(SHAKESPEARE,
KING LEAR, POOR QUARTO)

WHYNOT.

A cant word for violent or peremptory procedure.

'and snapped their canons with a whynot'   (HUD.)

'and snapped their EU membership with a whynot'
(BUD.)

WILL (OF THE PEOPLE).

Choice; arbitrary determination. Hence *will of the people*, arbitrary determination of the people, as persisting with Brexit, or so it is said.

'The wills above be done' (SHAKESPEARE, THE TEMPEST)

'*The wills of the people be done – or else*'
(SHAKESPEARE, THE BREXPEST)

WORM.

To deprive a dog of something (nobody knows what) under his tongue, which is said to prevent him (nobody knows why) from running mad.

So, to **BREWORM**, to deprive the populace of many things (nobody yet knows what) in order to prevent them from running mad.

WRETCHED.

Miserable. Unhappy.

'*These we should judge to be most miserable, but that a wretcheder sort there are.*'   (HOOKER)

'*the wretched mortals left behind*'   (WALLER)

Hence also **BREXCHED**, miserable to, for, by, with or from Brexit.

'*These we should judge to be most miserable, but that a Brexcheder sort there are.*'   (BOOHOOKER)

'*The Brexched mortals left behind in Brexit Britain.*'
(WAILER)

x.

A letter, which, though found in Saxon words, begins no word in the English language, and thus *Xenophobia*, a word which does not belong in English.

YEA.

[*ea*, Danish, German and Dutch] Yes. A particle of affirmation, consent and assent.

Hence too *Yea-rope*, that rope on which one pulls to sound a bell indicating approval or approbation or assent, and thus also *Yea-ropean*, one who thus rings the bell of approbation or assent.

YESTERDAY.

The day last past; a dimly recalled time much desired by those fearful of the future.

'if yesterday could be recall'd again' (DRYDEN)

'they did vote that yesterday be recall'd again'
(NEARLY-SWIFT)

Hence also **BREXSTERDAY**, the era past that some do yearn to restore through Brexit.

YOUNKER.

A young person, in contempt, as 'Foolish Younkers vote for Juncker!'
(THE DAILY DEPRESSED)

ZARNICH.

A solid substance in which orpiment is frequently found; and it approaches to the nature of orpiment, but without its lustre and foliated texture. Hence a very tough and stale sandwich, as previously served on British Rail and as promised under future legislation to renationalize the railways and the railway catering service.

ZEAL.

Passionate ardour for any person or cause.

'Zeal, the blind conductor of the will.'   (DRYDEN)

So, **BREX-ZEAL**, the blind and passionate ardour for Brexit.

A Note on Sources and Nomenclature

In harmony with the purposes of Johnson's English Dictionary, this volume... the years... upon finding the apter sounds and... phrases with which to represent its significance... the chosen words. It is the lasting glory and delight of the original compilation to display the riches of literature alongside those of the language... it is our aim to exhibit simple, relevant... the terms that have made the Age of Jewel... Indeed it is an age of great richness.

As Johnson, being the foremost Shakespearean of his time and indeed for all time, resorted in particular to the Bard for many of his supporting sentences, so a future writer have resorted to Shakespeare, but drawing upon the wealth of current scholarship we have been able to take our passages from the many more doubtful, dubious and dodgy folios and quartos of the immortal plays that have come to light

A Note on Sources
and Nomenclature

In harmony with the principles of Johnson's
English Dictionary, this volume sets great store
upon finding the aptest sources and quotations
with which to represent the signification of the
chosen words. It is the lasting glory and delight
of the original compilation to display the riches
of literature alongside those of the language;
it is our aim to exhibit similar riches alongside
the terms that have made the Age of Brexit feel
indeed like an age of great moment.

As Johnson, being the foremost Shakespearean of his time and perhaps of all time,
resorted in particular to the Bard for many of
his supporting sentences, so we in our turn have
resorted to Shakespeare, but drawing upon the
wealth of current scholarship we have been
able to take our passages from the many more
doubtful, dubious and dodgy folios and quartos
of the immortal plays that have come to light

under the eagle eyes of scholars. Alongside Shakespeare, Johnson also favoured the magisterial Elizabethan essayist Francis Bacon, whom some have continued to suspect of being the true author of the plays; by diligent sleuthery (which our critics will doubtless call sleight-of-hand) we have unearthed a number of his lesser disciples and descendants, including Francis Backon and Frank Rasher. We have also been able to benefit from some latterly discovered work by Shakespeare's boon companion Ben Jonson.

The great lexicographer also turned to the authors whom he admired in his own day and recent times, notably the poets John Dryden and Alexander Pope, the satirist and Dean of St Patrick's Cathedral Dublin, Jonathan Swift, and the founder of 'The Spectator' and indeed of periodical journalism, Joseph Addison. We have turned to their unjustly neglected counterparts, including John Drypen, Alexander Pop, Dean Not-So-Swift and Joseph Addidson, for our additional or supplementary passages, together with numerous other figures whose texts illuminate the riches of Brexit, including the shadowy and mystical Pseudo-Varoufakis. As Johnson was not afraid to pillage the news-sheets of his day, so we have also consulted 'Ye Daily Chain Mail', 'The Daily Depressed' and other voices of the town.

Being a dictionary of English and so fully illustrated from literary and other sources, Johnson's volume naturally includes many references to British history and its great characters, including notably Henry VIII and other monarchs. In our Brexit treasury, we similarly have found certain characters recurring in the passages used to explain or illustrate the words in their practical operation. Among the principal dramatis personae thus found displayed in the amber of the words are:

Sir Boris de Johnson, the most notable politicker and political scribbler of the age

Mistress May, sometimes also known as Good Mistress May, the national figurehead of the Age of Brexit

Master Nigel Shallow, an intriguer and stirrer with an apparent fondness for humble ale

Master Daffidavis, the chosen agent of Brexit in negotiations abroad

Monsieur Barmier, the much derided (among the news-sheets of the age around the town) appointed representative of France and other powers in those same negotiations

Ah Jeremy Corbyn, a prophetick and inspirational ringleader of hubbub and the forces of dis-may.

These and other notables of the Brexit time will be found preserved in the fragments of dubious Shakespeare folios and other literary and topical sources that illustrate our Brexit words. There will doubtless be some who object that while words are thankfully long, politicians are mercifully brief and so they should not be preserved in such a work of lasting reference. In response, we may note the somewhat overheated but otherwise pleasing remarks made by Alexander Pope, when he was criticized for referring to the transient names of his own day:

'Pretty! In amber to observe the forms
Of hairs, or straws, or dirt, or grubs, or worms;
The things, we know, are neither rich nor rare,
But wonder how the devil they got there.'

Thus it is that in recording for posterity the impact of Brexit on the life of the English language, and indeed of the language upon Brexit, we will inevitably also be preserving the names of some who have been most influential on public affairs and so frequently invoked that they appear to personify the spirit of the age. We trust that future readers for whom such figures are long lost will still enjoy the record of an episode in the unfolding life of our language, which will no doubt have been through many other phases by the time their eyes fall on these humble pages.